# Contract Law

I will be writing a brief synopsis on contract law in hopes that it may aid new paralegals on their  journey as Paralegals.  My  hope  is  that  when  you  become  "stuck"  on  any  of  the following topics that I will write about, that you will use this information as a guide

. This


has been a help for me though out the years,

and I hope that this information will be of

Help to you.

Cassandra Goode-Kitchen

# What is a Contract

A contract may be defined   as a promise,

or a set of promises, which obligates the parties to perform

As they have agreed

. If one of the parties fails to perform according to the contract,

. If one of the parties fails to perform according to the contract, then that party

may have breached the contract.

It may be helpful to think of a contract simply as an agreement between two or more parties.

A court may require the party in breach to perform

according to the contract or compensate

the innocent party for the value of the breach.

You are expected to honor contractual obligations

just as you are to meet the duty imposed by

Tort.  You are always obligated to "exercise reasonable  care  under  the  circumstances

. It is this

Voluntary aspect of contract law that sets it apart from "tort".

Being able to enter into a enforceable contract is one of our most important legal rights.

# Forming a contract

To form a contract between the parties, certain elements must be present.

These

Elements must be present in "All Contracts.

(1) Offer

(2)
(3) Acceptance

(4)

(5) Consideration

# A Voidable Contract

A voidable contract is not, nor is it completely valid

. When a contract is voidable, one

of the parties may elect whether or not to enforce the contract against the other party.

# Classification of Contracts

Whether a contract is valid, voidable,

or void, you must know how to classify the

contract based on other characteristics.

Not all contracts are formal, written, documents.

Many valid contracts as you know, are oral, rather than written.

Common sense dictates

That when possible,

a contract should be written so that parties can refer to its terms

# Acceptance

As a general rule,

an acceptance must be definite and must mirror the offer.

# Consideration

To find consideration in a contract,

both parties must bargain to give up something

Of value to n the other party,

which is sometimes termed " a legal detriment".

# Components  of  a  Contract

Remember,

most written contracts

will contain the following parts:

(1) Commencement

(2)

(3) Recitals (if any)

(4)
(5) Agreements

(6)
(7) Conclusion

(8)
(9)  Signatures

(10)

(11)

www.ingramcontent.com/pod-product-compliance
Lightning Source LLC
Chambersburg PA
CBHW080543190526
45169CB00007B/2613